I0517938

At the Still Point

A Play in Two Acts
by

Stephen Evans

For those who wait.

This is a work of dramatic fiction. The names, characters, places, and incidents are either the products of the author's imagination or are used fictitiously.

For production permissions and rights, contact: info@timebeingmedia.com

First Edition

ISBN: 978-1953725585

"The only way of catching a train that I have discovered is to miss the train before."

–G. K. Chesterton

STEPHEN EVANS

CONTENTS

STEPHEN EVANS

CAST OF CHARACTERS

GWEN   A Grace Kelly look-alike (more
              the actress than the princess
              despite her 60 years)

ART   Gwen's age, a writer, more
              William Powell than Robert
              Redford.

MERLE   The station vendor, who looks a
              little bit like the Princeton
              version of Einstein (sweatshirt
              and sneakers included).

Setting: A train station.

Time: Late.

STEPHEN EVANS

ACT I

Scene: A small train station. A few old benches are crowded together in the center. On the upstage wall is a round clock, the numbers, roman numerals, barely visible through the round crystal face, have delicate green vines climbing up them, twining around them. The time says 11:55 through most of the play. Upstage under the clock is a door to the train platform, with two old wooden chairs beneath. To the side is a cart for a vendor that offers newspapers, coffee, and various treats.

At Rise: MERLE sits doing a crossword puzzle behind the vendor cart, which is overflowing with various paraphernalia such as newspapers, souvenir hats, a carafe of coffee, various treats, and dust.

Merle glances up from his crossword and up at the round clock on the wall over the door leading to the tracks. He shakes his head. He has been looking up at that broken clock by habit for years.

Merle's gaze roves around the small circular station, over the few old, mismatched benches crowded together in a square, their differing lengths making a maze of paths through them, and which oddly all face away from the tracks.

Finally his gaze arrives at the only other occupant of the station. GWEN sits on the front bench, glancing occasionally back at the clock.

MERLE

Hey Lady.

Gwen turns around.

MERLE

What's an eight-letter word for unusual? Starts with a U. Not unusual. Well, unusual does. But unusual but not unusual. If you get me.

GWEN

Unwonted.

He counts it out.

MERLE
No, this one has an o in it.

GWEN
Unw<u>o</u>nted.

MERLE
Ah. Unwanted. Got ya.

He counts it out again.

MERLE
How do you spell that?

GWEN
(Spelling it out).
U-N-W-O-N-T-E-D. As in unwonted silence.

MERLE
Ah. Unwonted. Got ya. Thanks.

*She smiles and turns back. He goes back
to his crossword.*

MERLE
Hey Lady.

Gwen turns around again.

MERLE
When's your train?

GWEN

Soon.

She smiles and turns back.

GWEN

I hope.

MERLE

Want some coffee. On the house. Not much busy tonight.

Gwen turns around again.

GWEN

I don't drink coffee this time of night. But thanks.

She smiles and turns back. He goes back to his crossword.

MERLE

Snickers? Chips. I got chips. Gum. Cigarettes. Except you can't smoke in here.

Gwen turns around again.

MERLE

Used to. Used to you could smoke. Some days you could hardly breathe. I been here thirty-four years, right in this booth. Well, I mean I go home. But I've been working here thirty-

four years. I inherited from my uncle. He was
here twenty-seven years, right when they
opened this place.

GWEN
I imagine things have changed in thirty-four
years.

MERLE
You'd think so, wouldn't you?

> *She smiles and turns back. He goes back
> to his crossword.*

MERLE
Hey lady?

> *Gwen turns around again.*

GWEN
Mints. I'd like some mints.

> *Merle beams. He lives for this.*

MERLE
Stay there. I'll bring.

> *He walks down, hands her some mints,
> and sits. Gwen opens the package, takes
> one.*

MERLE
I'm Merle.

GWEN

Gwen.

MERLE

Thirty-four years I've worked here. Seven
more than my uncle. Beat him by seven. But
only because he died. So I don't brag about it.

GWEN

Mint?

MERLE

Sure. Thanks. Thirty-four years. I could have
retired. But what? I do the crossword at home?
Where is the sense in that?

He looks at her. After a second, she nods.

MERLE

Speaking of. I better get back to it. I like to
finish it by the time I leave.

GWEN

Good for you. I never finished one in my life.

Merle shrugs.

MERLE

If you don't stop, eventually you finish. You
have a good trip.

GWEN

Thank you.

He gets up and goes back to his cart. She spits out the mint.

ART walks through the station door, Gwen's age, more William Powell than Robert Redford.

He stops near to Merle's cart. but doesn't notice the vendor as he is scanning the room. Merle notices him, and his attention rises. Something unexpected is going to happen.

Art's gaze finally lands on Gwen and he stops dead still. Her back is to him, and all he can see is her golden hair. But he knows. Emotions flash across his face too fast to catalogue, and all of them come to rest at once.

Still, he does not move.

Gwen shifts in her seat, uneasily. Then she swivels and notices him.

Her expression undergoes a transition similar to his, but hers finishes in a smile.

He starts toward her.

*She watches him move, following him as
he moves toward her, not taking the path
around the wall of the station but cutting
through the maze, until he is standing in
front of her, the only last bench
intervening.*

GWEN

Art.

ART

Gwen.

*"Art and Gwen", they both think, for the
first time in many years. Art and Gwen
again. There is a power in the mythos of
those names, conjoined are a charm.*

GWEN

I didn't know if.

ART

It's not often I get an invitation from the past.

GWEN

Really? I get them all the time.

*He glides up the row of benches to where
she sits, their eyes never dropping
contact. As he rounds the bench, he trips
and almost falls, but catches himself.*

He grins.

She laughs.

Finally he is beside her.

They gaze for a moment.

ART
I was surprised to get your call.

GWEN
I was surprised you had the same phone number.

ART
Some things don't change.

GWEN
Most things do. Until they change back.

He gestures to the bench.

She nods, shifting her belongings to clear space.

He sits.

They gaze again.

Neither seems to know how to begin.

ART
So. What brings you back here?

GWEN
The funeral.

His mouth forms a oh.

ART
Not your Dad?

She shakes her head.

GWEN
No. He's still.

He laughs.

ART
I can imagine. I mean. Good for him. He must
be...

GWEN
93 last January.

*They are still for a moment. It is not
going the way either of them imagined.*

ART
So. Whose funeral?

GWEN
Izzy.

ART

Izzy. Who?

GWEN

She was in our class Senior year.

ART

Can't place her.

GWEN

She wasn't in our crowd.

ART

Ah. Did we have a crowd?

GWEN

More of gang. Gaggle. Pandemonium. Quiver.

ART

Quiver?

GWEN

Cobras.

ART

Ah.

He chuckles.

ART

That's about right.

Another pause.

> ART

I want to ask how the funeral was. But it sort of answers itself.

> GWEN

A lot of people there. I thought I might see you.

> ART

Didn't hear about it.

> *She looks surprised, then changes the subject, sort of.*

> GWEN

I think they should have funerals before you die. It seems rude to wait.

> ART

It does, doesn't it?

> GWEN

The nicest party you're ever invited to, and you really can't enjoy it.

> ART

Weddings are nice.

> *Her eyes widen.*

> ART

So I hear.

Now she is surprised.

GWEN

You never?

He shakes his head.

ART

You?

GWEN

Twice. No. Three times. Depends on how you count.

ART

Does it?

GWEN

You and Izzy should have gotten together.

He looks confused.

GWEN

I mean you live in the same small town. You'd think your paths would have crossed.

ART

I'm not much of a path-crosser. How about you?

GWEN

No. Except at funerals. And train stations.

Art looks around. Finally spots Merle in the corner who is studiously not paying attention to them while listening to every word.

He turns back.

ART
Is that why we're meeting here? You know you have a getaway scheduled?

GWEN
Maybe. And maybe I didn't want to spend my last minutes in this town with Merle.

ART
Who?

GWEN
Mint?

ART
Uh. Sure.

Gwen turns to Merle.

GWEN
Hey Merle.

MERLE
Yes, Milady?

GWEN

You still have that coffee you mentioned? We
could both use a cup.

MERLE

Sure.

*Excited by something to do other than the
crossword, he pulls out a carafe.*

Art smiles at her.

ART

You always had a penchant for making friends.

GWEN

You always had a penchant for using words
like penchant.

*He turns back and rests against the back
of the bench, not looking at her.*

ART

So.

GWEN

So.

ART

Why am I here?

GWEN

Going existential already. I thought you grew out of that phase in Twelfth Grade.

ART

Turtlenecks and dark glasses never go out of style.

Gwen reaches across him into her carry-on bag and pulls out a book.

GWEN

I finished your last book.

ART

Ah. You were the one who bought it.

GWEN

It reminded me of you.

ART

Hopefully that's a compliment.

GWEN

A not uncomplicated one, but yes.

ART

That's fair to say.

He takes the book, starts to flip the pages.

GWEN
It seemed like one of the characters might have been based on me.

ART
Maybe. In a not uncomplicated way.

GWEN
We had a not uncomplicated time together.

ART
We're not uncomplicated people.

He closes the book.

GWEN
Would you sign it for me?

ART
Sure. Do you have a pen?

GWEN
Oh.

She starts to search through her bag.

ART
Don't worry. I have one.

He pulls out a pen.

GWEN
Then why did you ask?

ART

In Author school, we're taught not to seem too
eager. It's an image thing.

*He signs it and hands it back. She reads it
and laughs.*

GWEN

To not uncomplicated memories. Funny.

ART

They teach us that too. And how to look
humble.

GWEN

Your handwriting has not improved.

ART

That they could not teach.

*She puts the book away, burying it in her
bag like treasure.*

GWEN

I kept your letters.

ART

From when we were together or from when
we weren't.

GWEN

Both.

ART
I'm surprised they haven't turned to dust. Or
been remaindered.

GWEN
Are you saying we're old and unwanted?

*Merle arrives behind them, bearing two
light blue paper cups of coffee with dark
plastic lids.*

MERLE
U-N-W-O-N-T-E-D. As in unwonted silence.
See I remember things.

*He hands each of them a cup. Art glances
at Gwen.*

GWEN
Crossword. Thank you, Merle.

*Merle draws packets of sweetener and
creamer out of seemingly every pocket
and dumps a bunch onto the bench
between them.*

MERLE
Sorry. It's been sitting a while.

GWEN
So have I.

MERLE
I can brew new!

GWEN AND ART
If only.

They smile.

GWEN
This is fine. We just need something to cover
the unwonted silences.

*Merle looks one to the other, and likes
what he sees.*

MERLE
Actually I don't brew myself. I get from the
coffee shop next door. It's good. So I'll go
borrow. You'll watch my cart?

GWEN
Like two hawks.

He hustles noisily out.

ART
Are you expecting any?

GWEN
Coffee?

ART
Unwonted silences.

GWEN
No, just the wonted ones.

They look at each other for a while.

She takes a drink.

He does too.

They grimace.

*They both add lots more cream and
sugar.*

ART
Well, I'm glad we got that out of the way.

GWEN
Me too.

He stands.

ART
Walk?

GWEN
I still get around.

He smiles.

ART
Would you like to take a walk?

GWEN
I would. But. My train should be here soon.

She glances at the clock.

GWEN
That's the theory anyway.

*He glances at the clock, then at her, then
back at the clock, then at his phone.*

GWEN
I think maybe it's the Doomsday clock. It
hasn't moved since I've been here, fortunately.

ART
Even a broken clock is right twice a day.

GWEN
Actually, a stopped clock is right twice a day.
A broken clock may never be right.

He looks at the clock again.

ART
Which do you think it is?

Gwen gazes up again, squinting a little.

GWEN
We'll have to wait and see.

ART
True.

Art turns to her. She returns the favor.

ART
Well, since we aren't facing imminent
Armageddon, how about a walk just around
the station?

GWEN
Take a turn around the room? How Jane
Austen of you.

ART
I'm nervous.

GWEN
Why?

ART
I haven't been up this late in about 30 years.

GWEN
There is that.

She stands.

GWEN
A turn it is.

She picks up the coffee cups.

GWEN
Shall we go armed?

*She hands his cup to him, then looks
around the station.*

GWEN
Clockwise or counterclockwise?

He glances at the clock.

ART
With this clock, I'm not sure there is a
difference.

GWEN
Good point. Left or right. Sunnyside or
widdershins? Upstream or downstream?

ART
Upstream. It's more literary.

GWEN
Born back ceaselessly into the past.

*She slips her free arm in his and begins to
stroll. He matches her stride instinctively.*

ART
Are you going far?

GWEN
Just once around. As far as I know.

ART
Are you traveling far?

GWEN
Still asking existential questions.

ART
I meant your train. Not prying. Just
wondering.

Gwen laughs.

GWEN
You had a penchant for that too.

ART
Wondering where you live now.

*At the end of the row of benches, Gwen
stops and takes a sip of coffee.*

She shrugs, getting used to the taste.

He does too.

He isn't, but he drinks anyway.

His lips press together in distaste.

*They laugh, then rotate in concert and
continue around the circular station.*

GWEN

I'm between homes at the moment.

*Art stops, and puts his hand on her arm,
which halts her as well.*

ART

You're homeless?

She shakes her head.

GWEN

No. I have five.

She starts walking again.

GWEN

I just don't know which to go to.

ART

Five homes?

He catches up.

ART

Why do you have five homes?

Gwen sighs.

GWEN

Two and a half husbands times two.

Gwen keeps going, but Art stops, doing the math in his head, never his strong point. But it seems right.

ART
You know you can sell them.

He catches up to her, again.

ART
You don't have to keep them forever.

Gwen stops. They are at the point in a meeting of old friends where some account of the years is required, and she is not sure that at whatever time at night it is that she has the energy.

She looks at him, her expression a mixture of longing for intimacy and a need for privacy.

But she can see that he will not accept the short answer.

She sighs.

GWEN
I hold onto them as a reminder of what I should never do again.

Art looks away, then back at her.

ART

That bad?

GWEN

Not in the living. Only in the remembering.

Arts nods.

Then shakes his head.

Then nods.

She smiles, wondering what mental process stimulated that sequence.

Art concludes his tortuous mental algorithm.

ART

I hate that.

GWEN

You too?

Art grimaces a bit.

ART

Sort of.

Realizing that they have entered another and likely uncomfortable phase of revelation, he guides her into a row of benches.

They shuffle in, careful not to spill or bump one another, then sit. His expression is distracted, hers full of curiosity.

ART
I'll write something.

GWEN
Seems like something a writer should do.

ART
You would think.

He shrugs.

ART
In the moment, I'll be convinced that it is the most brilliant thing I have ever written.

GWEN
And?

ART
And then I'll read it again later. In a year if I'm brave. In five if I'm not.

GWEN
Not as good?

ART
Never.

GWEN
Not even once?

ART
Not even.

GWEN
How odd.

They pause to be sure.

Then they laugh.

A sly look crosses over Art's face.

ART
Do you mind?

The old patter is beginning to reappear.

GWEN
I can't seem to help it.'

Art smiles.

ART
I don't want to pry.

GWEN
It's my own fault. I invited you.

ART
I'm just curious. Never having...

She takes a sip of coffee.

GWEN
I understand. Ask.

He does too.

No grimace this time.

He is too interested in other things.

ART
Divorced?

GWEN
One divorce, one widowing, one annulment.

He sits back, surprised.

ART
Annulment? They still do that?

GWEN
So my lawyer says.

He nods, absorbing.

ART

Why?

She looks away. Maybe embarrassed.

GWEN

He had another wife he forgot to mention.

Art nods again. Still absorbing.

ART

Ah. That's significant.

GWEN

Yes.

She stands, exits the aisle.

He follows.

They return to the stroll.

GWEN

It's not the good kind of threesome.

He stops, processing, then follows.

Catching up again.

ART

I'm starting to feel a bit provincial here.

Gwen shrugs.

GWEN

Small town.

She turns to him and smiles.

GWEN

And it's charming.

ART

Really?

Gwen laughs.

GWEN

Don't tell me you don't know.

ART

I could never tell with you, how you felt about things.

She lifts her hand, rescues him from some lint.

GWEN

As I recall, I made my feelings pretty clear.

He smiles.

ART

Well. That. Yes.

GWEN

A number of times.

                    ART
I remember.

> *Gwen rounds the last (or first) row of*
> *benches and pauses, looking out of the*
> *entrance (or exit) to the train platform in*
> *front of her.*

> *Through the double glass doors, the*
> *platform is lit only by a flickering*
> *fluorescent fixture, a Hopper painting*
> *flashing off and on.*

                    GWEN
I sometimes wonder. If. Back then. If you had
asked me to marry you—

> *She starts walking again. He follows*
> *slightly behind her, confused.*

                    ART
I did.

                    GWEN
You might have saved me two and a half
marriages and five houses I don't like.

                    ART
I did ask.

GWEN

Or maybe it would be three and a half
marriages and seven houses. Who knows?

ART

I did ask you.

GWEN

Life takes these funny turns. Except I never
seem to laugh.

ART

Gwen. I did ask you to marry me.

*She stops underneath the recalcitrant
clock and looks up.*

*The clock face is reflected in the
darkened window across the station,
though the wall on which it hangs is not
itself visible in the reflection, so the clock
appears suspended in the air.*

*The hanging lights also hang suspended
in the reflection like stars around the
moon).*

*And in the reflection, the hands of the
mirrored clock are turning now, but
backwards.*

Gwen steps out a pace and glances up at the actual clock. The hands are where they have been. Motionless.

Art joins her, also looking up. He sees the clock, turns and gives her a questioning glance.

She steps back against the wall, tilts her head and squints a bit.

The illusion in the mirror resolves: the hands once more are still.

                    ART
What?

Gwen shakes her head.

                    GWEN
Nothing.

Then his words finally register with her.

She looks at him in shock.

Amusement replaces confusion in his expression.

                    GWEN
You did what?

Art nods.

ART
I did ask you to marry me.

Long pause.

They both take a sip of coffee.

Gwen looks around.

There are two ancient wooden chairs to the left of the track door, just under the clock.

She sits, sending her memory on a quest.

GWEN
Are you sure?

He laughs, sits in the other chair.

ART
I'm positive.

Now it is Gwen's head that twists, first one way, then the other.

GWEN
Were we stoned?

He shakes his head.

GWEN

It doesn't count if you're stoned.

ART

We were not stoned. It counted for me. The one and only.

She looks at him.

GWEN

No.

He nods his head.

GWEN

You're not joking?

ART

No.

GWEN

And it wasn't a joke then? That we maybe just laughed off.

His eyes narrow, remembering. Then he turns and looks at her.

ART

I did not laugh it off.

She still can't grasp it.

GWEN
Because we were only?

ART
I was 21. You were.

GWEN
(Quickly)
Younger. Hmmm. Really? Wow.

She looks at him with a wry smile.

GWEN
Maybe I didn't like you as much as I remember.

ART
Apparently.

Gwen sips.

He still does not.

GWEN
Was I nice about it at least?

Art's lips come together, as he tries to decide how to characterize the moment.

Then he nods, slowly, as if coming to a conclusion he had not known before.

                    ART
You were. Sort of. You pretended it didn't
happen.

                    GWEN
What?

                    ART
You went on talking about going to Europe for
the summer.

                    GWEN
Really?

    She frowns.

                    GWEN
I said nothing?

    *He slides his hand along the back of her
    chair.*

                    ART
Not about that.

    *His hand twitches a bit, wanting to touch
    her hair. But his fingers curl into a fist
    instead.*

    *Instead, she leans her head back,
    trapping his arms there.*

ART

You talked about how you heard Prague was
so beautiful and you couldn't wait to see the
Volga.

GWEN

Vltava.

ART

Gesundheit.

She sits up and shoots him a look.

GWEN

Funny. The Vltava flows through Prague.

ART

I didn't know that then.

GWEN

Probably neither did I.

*Art retrieves his hand from behind her
chair.*

ART

So we finished our dinner and I took you
home.

*Gwen is still lost in the struggle to recall
any of the episode.*

Finally.

GWEN
Did we break up?

He shakes his head.

ART
Not till you went to Europe that summer.

She turns to him, with pseudo-anger to cover a growing and unexpected sense of remorse.

GWEN
A woman turns down your proposal of marriage and you still date her? What, have you no self-respect?

Art shrugs.

ART
The sex was really good.

Gwen stares at him.

Then shrugs herself.

Then laughs.

GWEN
Oh. Well. Sure. You're a man.

She turns back and leans against the

slatted back of the chair, her head hitting against the ancient wall, forgetting he had moved his arm.

She frowns.

GWEN
Wait. Where did this alleged proposal take place?

ART
Jake's Crab House.

Gwen laughs. Loudly.

GWEN
You're kidding. Did you want me to say no?

Now Art glares.

ART
Of course not.

He unfolds his arms, open his hands.

ART
I thought it was romantic.

GWEN
You thought Jake's Crab House was romantic?

> ART

We had been there several times. I thought of it as our place.

She sees he is serious but can't help laughing.

> GWEN

You thought Jake's Crab House was our place?

> ART

Apparently. At the time.

She laughs again.

> GWEN

Then I think we need a new place.

> ART

Do we?

> GWEN

I'm sure of it.

She looks at him intently, curious again.

> GWEN

Did you want me to say yes?

> ART

Probably.

He smiles.

ART
I doubt that I thought through the alternatives.

Gwen shrugs again.

GWEN
Oh. Well. Sure. You're a man.

*Now she crosses her arms, gives him a
searing and skeptical look.*

GWEN
So you proposed to me at the noisiest
restaurant on the East Coast.

He nods.

GWEN
Did you get down on one knee?

He thinks.

ART
No.

*She gestures as if to say, what do you
expect?*

ART
It was a crab house. The floor was a mess.

She can't help herself.

She laughs loudly, for a long time.

She gets herself under control.

She starts again.

He joins her this time.

He remembers this laugh.

He always loved it.

GWEN
Understandable.

They calm down.

GWEN
Was there a ring?

ART
There was. But I never got to that part.

Gwen hums a bit, pondering, looking up.

GWEN
So I have a theory.

Art's expression scrunches, and he sighs.

ART
Don't say it.

GWEN
You know what it is?

He nods.

ART
I think so.

> *Gwen spins her body toward him again,*
> *and reaches out her non-coffee hand to*
> *touch his cheek. Then slaps him slightly.*
> *Just the merest touch.*

GWEN
I don't think I heard you.

> *He closes his eyes.*

> *He has thought about that moment many*
> *times over the years, always coming to*
> *the same conclusion.*

ART
I don't think you did either.

> *Long pause.*

> *They lean back into the wall.*

> *Both take a sip. Or try. But the coffee is*
> *gone.*

Art takes the cups, walks to a trash can, deposits, returns, and sits.

Gwen twists and slides closer to him, resting against his shoulder.

GWEN

Wow.

ART

I know.

GWEN

I mean.

ART

I know!

GWEN

Wow.

ART

I know.

Moments pass.

Gwen revolves and looks into his eyes, so curious to see what she can see there.

Mostly, there is humor.

Then she looks deeper, seeing the wonder at the question of the evening, the question she now cannot stop thinking about herself: what if?

And behind that wonder, she sees understanding, that they have each travelled their own paths, and that those paths have brought them here.

And somehow here in the station beneath the stopped or broken clock the question in both their minds is transformed, from what if?, to what now?

And they both realize that, but neither knows how to face it, or answer it.

                    GWEN
Can you imagine?

                    ART
Vividly.

He closes his eyes, remembering.

                    ART
Every day.

Then opens them, smiles at her.

                    ART
For several years.

Gwen reaches up, patting his check
again, nicely this time.

GWEN

Poor boy.

ART

I had even spoken to your father beforehand.

She swivels to him, though it isn't as easy
on the chairs as on the benches. She pulls
the edge of her skirt to straighten it.

GWEN

No!

ART

Yep. In my 20-year-old classic nerd mind, it
was the right thing to do.

She swivels back, laughs, then back to
him.

GWEN

What did my father say?

Art looks at her with a pained smile as if
to say: you know your father, what do you
think he said?

ART

He said good luck. In that way he had of
saying, no way in hell but I respect you for
asking anyway.

She chuckles.

GWEN

Yes. He could say a lot in a few words. Can
say.

ART

He never told you about it?

GWEN

Never told, never asked.

Art nods.

GWEN

He liked you. He never said it. But he did. I
could tell.

ART

Sure. He looked at me and thought: here is a
boy who will never leave this town. And who
could keep my Gwen here with him. And he
was right, about the first part. I don't think
anyone could have kept you here though.

GWEN

No.

ART
Did you ever think about moving back?

GWEN
No.

Art nods.

ART
Didn't think so.

Gwen takes his hand.

GWEN
I mean.

She shakes her head, trying to imagine.

GWEN
Our whole lives could have been different.

She takes his hand in both of hers, pulls it to her.

GWEN
Our whole lives.

ART
Yes.

He nods.

ART

Maybe.

He takes back his hand.

ART

But who knows? Lives change every minute.
From the choices we make.

GWEN

Like restaurant selection.

He laughs.

ART

Like restaurant selection. And from the
choices we don't even think of as choices. Like
asking me here.

She looks at him, questioning.

GWEN

Like coming here?

ART

That too.

GWEN

I knew I was making a choice. After all these
years, I knew.

ART

So did I.

GWEN
What was the deciding factor?

ART
I suppose. Curiosity.

GWEN
Me too!

Gwen laughs, sighs, laughs again.

GWEN
It's mind boggling.

ART
It is.

She sets her shoulders.

GWEN
So.

ART
Yes?

GWEN
How long?

ART
Yes?

GWEN
How long have you held this theory that I
never heard you?

*He reaches for coffee, then realizes there
isn't any. He looks to the entrance for
Merle. No sign. Then shrugs.*

ART
Since the next day.

Gwen is astonished.

GWEN
That's a long time.

ART
Almost—

GWEN
Oh let's not.

ART
Agreed.

*Gwen works her way through vague
memories of the evening.*

GWEN
Why didn't you say anything?

*Now Art laughs loudly. In the empty
station it reverberates, almost an echo
but not quite—more a remembrance of
laughter lost.*

ART
What was I supposed to say? Oh by the way,
did you hear my proposal of marriage?

GWEN
I see the problem.

ART
I did not want to go through it again.

*She crosses her arms, slightly more of an
interrogative.*

GWEN
Even though you may not have gone through it
the first time?

He barks a rueful laugh.

ART
I went through it. Apparently you didn't.

GWEN
I suppose.

*He crosses his arms over his chest, as if
defending himself.*

ART

It was the most soul-crushing experience of
my entire life. I was devastated.

He glances at her, then away.

ART

You know.

GWEN

Know what?

ART

At that age. How you feel things.

*Gwen performs her sort-of chuckle again,
and leans her head against his shoulder.*

GWEN

That I remember.

*She turns and puts a hand where her
head had rested.*

GWEN

I'm so sorry.

He sighs.

ART

Thank you. Though.

She raises up, looks at him.

GWEN

Yes?

ART

I am curious.

GWEN

So you said.

ART

I suppose that's why I came.

GWEN

Then ask.

He squints a bit, pauses.

ART

Now I'm not sure I want to know.

She nods, understanding.

ART

I mean. Is it worth knowing, while knowing
that it changes nothing?

*She pulls her hand back and thinks. This
is an inflection point, she realizes.*

GWEN

It changes nothing that has happened.

He puts his head back against the wall, in relief or frustration, or both.

GWEN

But.

He raises his head and looks at her.

GWEN

you don't know that it would change nothing in the future.

He is listening now.

GWEN

Or even

He is listening harder.

GWEN

The now.

She looks at him.

He raises a finger, as if about to proclaim something grand.

ART

Now that is existential.

She laughs, but is slightly annoyed at his deflection.

ART
You must have learned it from me.

GWEN
Possibly.

*He pulls down his finger, and his
expression goes serious.*

ART
At the still point, there the dance is.

GWEN
Excuse me?

ART
T. S. Eliot.

She nods knowingly.

GWEN
I thought so.

She smiles.

GWEN
For a moment, I thought you were asking me
to dance.

ART
Only at the still point.

She looks around.

GWEN
It doesn't get more still than this.

ART
True. There's no music.

GWEN
The sound comes and goes. The music is
always real.

ART
Who said that?

GWEN
You did. In one of your novels.

ART
Did I? Good line.

He turns to her and offers her his hand.

They dance.

There is no music.

They don't seem to mind.

Lights fade.

End Act 1.

STEPHEN EVANS

ACT II

Scene:	The same small train station. The clock is still broken.
At Rise:	Gwen and Art dance back and forth, in and out of the lights and shadow, from the overhead lights.

Art breaks away and sits. She joins him.

GWEN

That was nice. I didn't mind no music.

ART

My heart was beating like a drum. Does that count?

GWEN

It was nice. Familiar. It reminded me.

ART

Yes?

GWEN

That you were a terrible dancer.

ART

True. But when I danced with you, no one was looking at me.

He takes her hand again.

GWEN

Another try?

He wonders what she is asking there.

ART

Not exactly.

He places his other hand over hers.

GWEN

You're not going to propose again, are you?

ART

No. Are you disappointed?

She thinks a bit.

GWEN

Possibly. I've had several, but I am curious
how you would go about it.

ART

Not well, apparently. Considering.

GWEN

True. But maybe you learned something from
the first attempt.

ART

I don't think this is something where
experience is a help.

GWEN

True. It didn't help me, I can say that. So if
you're not proposing, what do you want to
know?

He pauses, decides to go ahead and ask.

ART

If you had heard? When I proposed?

GWEN

Yes?

Art draws out the sentence.

ART

What do you think you would have said?

Gwen hesitates.

GWEN

Mint?

Art mock scowls.

ART

Oh come on. I've waited mphmfh years for an
answer.

She shakes her head.

GWEN
How could I possibly know now what I would
have felt then if?

ART
I know how I felt.

GWEN
How?

*He moves to the bench opposite her and
sits.*

*He looks up at the stopped or broken
clock.*

Then he pulls out his wallet.

*In an almost ritualistic fashion, he slides
his reading glasses out of his pocket.*

Clears his throat.

Turns sightly away from her.

ART

I felt that no one else in the world could wear a baseball cap as well as you. I felt that when you jogged by my house in the morning with your ponytail swinging side to side that the earth spun a little slower just to give me more time to gaze at you in wonder. I felt that when you shook your hair a certain way there was air to breathe. I felt that when my arms were around you I didn't need the air anymore and when your hand was in mine my heart didn't need to beat. I felt that when you passed by flowers leaned your way and the grass turned greener just for you. I felt that your silhouette just filled the empty space in my life like one of those cartoon cutouts. I felt that when you smiled a butterfly must be born somewhere because that much beauty must have consequences.

Gwen takes a moment.

So much clicks into place.

GWEN

That's how you felt?

ART

Yes.

She nods, taking it all in, recalibrating.

GWEN
Was that how you proposed?

He laughs.

ART
No.

He takes a moment, to see if he can remember exactly.

ART
I think. When I proposed. I said something like: I think we should get married. Don't you?

GWEN
That's what you said?

He can't look at her.

He wonders if after this revelation he will ever be able to look at her again.

Then he wonders if, after tonight, he will ever get another chance.

ART
There may have been an extra pause or two, but pretty much.

GWEN

But that other, the baseball cap and the
running.

ART

Jogging.

GWEN

And the grass and the butterfly. You
remember all that.

ART

I do.

GWEN

How?

ART

I wrote it down.

*He takes out his wallet and unfolds a
ragged piece of paper.*

ART

First bit of writing I ever did.

She reaches for it.

*He doesn't let it go at first, but finally he
does.*

She stares at the unfolded paper.

GWEN
And you kept it. All this time.

ART
Sort of.

GWEN
What do you mean—sort of?

Art reaches for it.

She doesn't want to let it go, but she does.

ART
Well. I look at it once in a while.

GWEN
You look at it.

ART
After a few years, it wears out. So I retype it. I still have my old typewriter and I found some of the same notepaper. So it looks the same.

Gwen reaches for the paper again, but he doesn't give it to her.

GWEN
How many times have you retyped it?

ART
I don't know.

GWEN

Give me a ballpark number.

Art sighs again.

ART

Eight.

GWEN

Eight.

ART

Eight.

GWEN

So did you keep it because it was your first real piece of writing or because it reminded you of how you felt about me.

ART

The first one.

GWEN

Oh.

ART

I didn't need anything to remind me how I felt about you.

He sighs.

ART

And then I didn't want anything to remind me.

He nods.

ART
And then it didn't remind me. Because I found
I had it memorized.

GWEN
So I see.

ART
And then.

GWEN
Yes?

ART
And then it occurred to me that it was really
good and I should use it. So I did. In a book.

GWEN
The one I just read.

ART
That's the one. That's what we authors do. We
put things in books. And we try to disguise
them, so no one knows who they are about.

GWEN
That was the passage, when I read it, I thought:
is that me?

ART
Except sometimes the people they are about.

. GWEN

It made me curious. I think that's why I called.
Maybe.

They both pause, exhausted.

GWEN

What took you so long?

ART

Excuse me?

GWEN

What took you so long? To put it in a book.

ART

It nearly when into every book I wrote. But I
always took it out. Until this one.

GWEN

Why this one?

ART

Because I could finally bear it.

*He holds the paper up to the light. The
light shines through it, highlighting the
words. He folds it again.*

ART

Gwen.

> GWEN

Yes?

> ART

Would you?

> GWEN

Marry you? I heard that one.

He laughs.

> ART

Would you like to have it?

> GWEN

You don't want it anymore?

> ART

I put it in a book. It's not mine now.

> GWEN

Ah. Okay. Thanks. I would like to have it.

He hands it to her. She holds it up.

> GWEN

Might be worth something someday, the first piece of writing by a famous novelist.

> ART

You never know.

> GWEN

I never did.

There is a long pause. They both sense disappointment seeping in, as if they have passed the turning point but did not turn.

Merle enters.

They don't notice.

He watches for a moment, assessing.

Then he bustles up noisily, carafe in one hand, fresh cups in the other.

MERLE
Looks like I'm just in time.

He hands each of them a round clear mug, like a glass ball with the top open, then pours the liquid carefully into Gwen's cup.

MERLE
Coffee, fresh.

He pours into Art's cup.

MERLE
There. Now you're ready for another unwonted silence.

GWEN
You're really liking that word, aren't you?

*Merle again unloads handfuls of creamer
and sugar packets onto the bench.*

MERLE
Why do you think I do crosswords?

More sugar.

MERLE
You're never too old.

More creamer.

MERLE
Well, that's not true. Sometimes you are.

More multi-colored packs of sweetener.

MERLE
But you're never too old to think you're never
too old.

*Gwen smiles at him, genuine, and
amused.*

GWEN
Thank you, Merle.

*Merle assumes a superhero mission
accomplished pose.*

MERLE
It's what I'm here for.

ART

Yes, thank you. Our silences are now covered for the remainder of the evening. Morning. Whichever time this is.

Merle unposes, goes back to his cart.

Gwen and Art look at each other for a moment.

They take a long sip without losing eye contact, then simultaneous smiles of delight.

Neither adds anything extra to the cup.

Gwen swivels toward Merle.

GWEN

This is delicious. Thank you, Merle. Just what we needed.

Merles waves away the praise.

Art stands, holds out his non-coffee hand to Gwen.

ART

Shall we?

She takes his hand and stands.

GWEN

We shall.

> *They walk in contented silence, glad to
> have said things that long needed saying.*
>
> *At the end of the first row of benches,
> they reach Merle's cart.*
>
> *Merle, who has returned to his
> crossword, does not look up, diligently
> chanting the words to himself.*
>
> *Gwen and Art make it down the aisle
> about halfway, when Gwen glances back
> at Merle, then sighs.*

GWEN

Must be nice.

ART

What?

GWEN

To know what you're here for.

ART

You're here for a funeral.

> *Gwen catches his eye again, looks
> intently for a moment, then sighs again.*

GWEN

Am I?

ART

Aren't you?

GWEN

I suppose.

They start walking again.

GWEN

A funeral.

Walking.

GWEN

A commemoration.

Walking.

GWEN

Of loss.

She stops.

GWEN

And passage.

She turns around.

GWEN

Hey Merle, what's another word for funeral?

MERLE
(Without looking up)
Exequy.

Gwen is impressed.

GWEN
How about a word for funeral song?

MERLE
(Still without looking up)
Epicedium.

Gwen nods.

GWEN
Yes. That's why I'm here. An epicedium.

MERLE
(Still without looking up)
Your crossword is depressing.

Gwen laughs.

GWEN
It is, isn't it?

They start walking again.

ART
You're in a pensive mood.

GWEN
Is that the right word? Pensive?

ART
It must be. I'm a writer.

GWEN
Then I guess I am. No. I wouldn't say pensive.

ART
What would you call it?

GWEN
I don't think I'd call it anything.

ART
I see.

*At the final turn, they swing around
towards the place where they began,
marked by the bag and the book.*

GWEN
If I call my mood something, it will send it off
in one direction or another. And this mood is
something that needs to go where it's going
and I need to wait until it gets there. Like my
train.

Having reached her seat, Gwen hesitates.

ART
Would you like me to wait with you?

Gwen looks at him intently, and if he didn't know better he would have said she was sticking her tongue out at him.

But he does know better.

GWEN
As it turns out, I would like that very much.

He smiles.

They sit in their original places and set their empty cups to the side, eyes never straying during the descent.

GWEN
I never drink coffee this late. Now I'll be up all night. Which might be just as well considering how late my train may or may not be.

Art laughs.

ART
Why the train? Just curious.

GWEN
I always travel by train.

ART
Why?

GWEN

Why? I don't know. I like the getting there.
Instead of just the arriving.

Art nods.

ART

I like the train too.

GWEN

Really? Why?

ART

They travel in lines. No arcs. No parabolas
through the sky. No short cuts across the
earth. Here to there. I'm a here-to-there kind
of guy.

GWEN

You always were.

ART

Was I? I don't think of myself that way.

She shakes her head.

GWEN

You always were. Trust me.

Art says nothing for a moment.

ART

How about you?

GWEN
Here to there? Not so much.

GWEN
Or. I don't know. Maybe. In a not
uncomplicated way.

ART
I meant. Are you what you always were?

GWEN
What do you think?

Art laughs.

She likes this laugh, deep and genuine.

ART
With you? I think there is no past tense.

GWEN
More likely subjunctive.

ART
If only that were true.

Gwen laughs, then frowns at him.

GWEN
You're a writer. It's your job to know these
things.

Art laughs. They have a rhythm going.

Then he sighs.

ART

The more I write, the more I think my job is
not to know anything.

GWEN

Stop writing.

ART

Now there, past tense is appropriate.

*Gwen puts her hand on his forearm and
pulls him around to her.*

GWEN

You can't stop writing.

ART

Why not?

GWEN

How will we know what happens next?

*Art pats her hand, slips his fingers under
it and holds it.*

ART

Maybe nothing will.

She kisses him.

                    GWEN
You never know.

    He nods.

                    ART
You never do.

                    GWEN
So you don't like past tense and you don't like
subjunctive and you don't like future tense.
What will you write?

                    ART
Screenplays.

    She thinks.

                    GWEN
I could see that.

                    ART
Conditional. Story of my life.

    He turns to her.

                    ART
Are you okay?

        *Gwen takes her time in answering, both
        to decide what to tell, and to decide what
        the answer is. It is such a simple
        question—and like most such questions it*

does not have a simple answer.

GWEN

I'm alive.

ART

Is that an answer?

GWEN

It's the only answer I know.

Art pauses, wondering if he should pursue it, wondering if he has the right to know more, wondering if she is right that it is the only answer.

ART

Okay, what shall we do while we wait?

Gwen pauses, realizing that their conversation has now become punctuated by time.

GWEN

Let's talk about you.

ART

Me? That is a very short story. I hope you don't have long to wait.

Gwen smiles.

GWEN

According to the clock, I haven't been waiting at all.

ART

I mean, there's not much to tell. I live in the town I grew up in. And I write books.

GWEN

Never married?

ART

No. I proposed once.

She grimaces.

GWEN

Sorry. Children?

ART

Yes, actually.

Gwen is surprised.

GWEN

Really? You scoundrel you.

Art chuckles.

ART

Yes, that's me. Scoundrel.

GWEN

Blackguard.

ART

Rascal.

GWEN

Dastard.

ART

Excuse me? Oh, dastard. I like the sound of
that actually.

Gwen puts her hand on his.

GWEN

Okay, enough literary posturing. Tell me the
story.

ART

I'm not sure I can tell a story without literary
posturing. I'd be thrown out of the Literary
Fiction guild. We're very self-important.

GWEN

Just this once. Between us and Merle.

He sighs, leans back against the bench.

ART

I was living with someone. We weren't
married. And she had a child. who was sharp
and bright, and funny, and. And wise. Wiser
than I was. And I adored her. So I unofficially
adopted her.

GWEN
And her mother?

ART
Her mother and I split up after a couple of years. But. She's still my daughter. She lives on the West Coast now. But when she comes east, I get to see her.

Gwen smiles.

GWEN
See. Was that so hard?

ART
I'll let you know after the next guild meeting.

Gwen leans against his shoulder, relaxes into him.

GWEN
You're lucky.

ART
I know. You?

Gwen sighs.

GWEN
Not lucky. Not in that way.

ART
I'm sorry.

Gwen sits up again.

GWEN

I am too sometimes. But. Not often. It's like.
Do you miss being able to leap tall buildings at
a single bound? Well, no, it sounds nice, but I
never had it in my life, so I don't miss it. I
wonder sometimes what it would have been
like. But even that, not often. Did you want
kids?

Art laughs.

ART

Never occurred to me, honestly. Until it
happened.

GWEN

I think.

*She turns to him. The loss of the tiny
pressure of her head against his shoulder,
leaves him bereft.*

GWEN

I think that is the way life should be. We
shouldn't say life is meaningless without—
whatever. Life is never meaningless, because it
was never meant to be meaningful. That's us,
that's our culture, our parents, our teachers
telling us. But it's not true. We have no idea

what life is supposed to be, because it's not supposed to be anything. Our species is a few hundred thousand years old, our language is far younger than that. How can we possibly think we have the words to explain life? Maybe some species billions of years from now. But I doubt it.

                    ART
See. Pensive.

                    GWEN
No. Just a lot of time to read on the train. Okay. Maybe. So. No marriages. One child. How many books have you written?

                    ART
23.

                    GWEN
Don't get out much, do you?

                    ART
Visits from old friends are few and far between.

    Gwen smiles and pats his face again.
    Then smacks him lightly.

                    GWEN
That's for using the O word.

She reaches into her bag and pulls out his book again.

GWEN
I thought I had read them all, but I haven't read anywhere near 23.

She turns to the inside flap.

GWEN
It lists six here.

ART
Only six of them are published.

GWEN
Six? Why? You're so good.

ART
Thank you. It's the way of the publishing world. Six published is good. Six is a lot.

Gwen looks at the book again.

GWEN
Wow. So you have seventeen books sitting in a drawer.

ART
Actually, they're in the Cloud, but yes, metaphorically speaking.

GWEN

Are they good?

Art thinks about his answer.

ART

They are—well-written.

GWEN

That sounds like a no.

ART

They aspire to sound like good books.

Gwen looks at him.

GWEN

I'd like to read them.

Art laughs, shakes his head.

ART

I don't think...

He stops.

GWEN

What?

ART

I don't think I want you to remember me as the person who wrote them.

GWEN

Why is that important?

ART

I don't know. It wasn't an hour ago. An hour ago, I would have been happy for anyone to ask to read them. Though I still would have probably said no. I haven't read most of them in years. I can't vouch for them, I guess I am saying.

GWEN

I can see that. I get it. Still. 23 books in mphmfh years. That's an accomplishment.

Art laughs again, and she sees that this is his standard response to praise. And somehow that makes her sad, that he should think so little of something she admires so much.

ART

Of a sort, I suppose.

GWEN

It's impressive to me. I struggle with Christmas cards.

Now he shrugs. Back to the shrug, which is not as dismissive somehow as the laugh.

ART

So do I.

GWEN

Really? So. One thing we have in common.

ART

Meant for each other.

GWEN

Absolutely. We were meant to not write
Christmas cards together until the end of time.

*He shrugs again. But somehow it has
changed, she thinks. Somehow it is
Amused. Even Hopeful.*

ART

It's something.

GWEN

Not exactly Heathcliff and Cathy.

*His eyebrows climb half an inch on his
face.*

ART

It's the 21st century equivalent.

GWEN

Hmm. This does seem to be an unromantic
century so far.

ART
There's still time.

GWEN
For the century, true.

ART
And for us.

GWEN
You think so?

ART
I'm not ready to rule it out.

GWEN
By us, do you mean you and me or do you
mean us?

ART
I mean you and me.

She nods.

ART
But I'm not ruling out us. We are having
delicious coffee alone in a train station. That
seems potentially romantic.

GWEN
Only to a romantic. Makes me wonder about
those unpublished books.

She eyes him quizzically. Then shrugs.

The new shrug, not the old one.

ART

Ask.

GWEN

Did they have happy endings?

He pauses, thinking through them. It takes a while—he can barely remember some of their titles.

ART

I suppose you could say that. In a Dante-ish sort of way.

Gwen picks up his book, stares at it, weighs it in her hand, and flips through the pages, placing her hand palm down on some as though she is trying to absorb by osmosis.

GWEN

Who is your favorite writer?

ART

Other than me?

She looks up.

GWEN

Other than you.

ART

Actually, we don't have to exclude me. There are many books I'd rather read than mine.

GWEN

It's not the same thing, is it?

ART

What do you mean?

Gwen closes the book decisively, the better to argue her point.

GWEN

Books you'd rather read is different from favorite writer.

GWEN

Art?

ART

Gwen?

GWEN

Are you okay? Not having a heart attack, are you?

ART

My heart is fine.

GWEN

Good. Because I don't know CPR. I do know the Heimlich Maneuver.

ART

Noted.

GWEN

No. They are not the same.

ART

The Heimlich Maneuver is not the same as CPR?

GWEN

No, a book you want to read most is not the same as favorite writer. Because a book you would rather read is affected by other factors, like how tired you are or what mood you're in.

GWEN

Favorite writer is the writer whose books mean the most to you.

ART

Oh. Well. Then I am my favorite writer, but I'd rather read anyone else's books instead of mine.

GWEN

Why?

ART

I don't know about other writers, but by the time I finish one of mine I am sick of it. The

only page of it I want to open is the one I sign
my name to at a bookstore. Or train station.

GWEN
Your books, the published ones anyway, are
warm and entertaining and thoughtful. I like
them very much.

ART
Thank you for the blurb. I'll add it to my
marketing material. You are my target
demographic.

GWEN
You mean women of a certain age?

ART
No. I mean you. I always write for you.
Though I'm not sure if it's the you I remember
or the you I imagine.

GWEN
Really. Well. Good job.

ART
Thank you.

Gwen puts down the book.

*He notices, and knows he has lost a
chance. He would not have the courage
now. They have achieved something, and*

*he fears he would disturb it, cancel it,
whatever it is.*

GWEN
No one's ever written anything for me before.
Much less 23 books. Wait, that's not true. I got
a postcard once. But it was from my mother.

ART
What did it say?

GWEN
It didn't say anything. I suppose it was meant
to be sort of proof of life.

*Art lifts his head to the ceiling, thinking
this through.*

ART
I think that's what my books are. Proof of life.

Gwen nudges him with her shoulder.

GWEN
It's better than a postcard.

ART
In scale.

Gwen nudges him again.

GWEN
Now you're just being modest.

Art lowers his head, looks at her.

ART
They teach that at Author School too.

*She turns, climbing up and kneeling on
the bench, her white shoes barely
revealed under her lavender dress.*

GWEN
Hey Merle. Who's your favorite author?

*Merle finishes a word and puts down the
crossword.*

MERLE
My favorite or the one I like to read most?

*Gwen gives Art her fabled I-Told-You-So
glance.*

GWEN
Who's your favorite?

*Merle goes back to his crossword, pencils
in another line.*

MERLE
Tolstoy.

GWEN
Really?

MERLE
In Russian. You have to read Tolstoy in
Russian.

GWEN
You speak Russian?

MERLE
Ya uznal ot babushki. Ona by ne vyuchila
angliyskiy.

GWEN
Ya ne vinyu yeye.

Merle nods.

MERLE
You speak Russian.

GWEN
Da.

Art turns and kneels on the bench.

ART
Hey Merle. Why Tolstoy?

MERLE
I only read one book a year, so it needs to last.

ART
There's Proust.

MERLE
I don't drink tea.

ART
Joyce.

MERLE
Juvenile sense of humor.

ART
And you find Tolstoy funny?

MERLE
In Russian, he's hilarious.

ART
So Tolstoy. Fine choice. War and Peace?

MERLE
That's good. But I prefer Anna Karenina.

GWEN
Me too.

Art glances at her.

GWEN
Has trains in it.

ART
True. Not a happy ending though.

GWEN
You'll just have to write your version.

Pause. They drink. She looks at the clock, shakes her head.

ART
Why don't they fix that clock?

Art looks at it. He gets up and walks toward it, stands under it for a moment.

ART
Hey Merle?

MERLE
Yeah?

ART
Why don't they fix that clock?

MERLE
Cause everybody has a phone now. Nobody even looks at it nowadays.

Art stares up at the clock.

ART
Hey Merle?

MERLE
Yeah?

ART
Have you got a ladder?

Gwen rises.

GWEN

Art?

ART

Gwen?

She smiles.

This look she knows, this intensity. She had never had a problem getting men's attention, though often getting men's attention was a problem in itself. But she remembered his face when he looked at her that way; as though he saw her completely, and through her completely. And in doing so, he also opened all of himself to you. When you were the object of that all-encompassing attention, it was unnerving, and exciting.

GWEN

Don't hurt yourself.

ART

I'm just going to reset it. Maybe that will get it started. Where's the ladder, Merle?

MERLE

In the closet. But I'm not sure it's tall enough.

> ART

We'll see.

*Art goes to the closet and pulls out a
ladder.*

*Merle wanders over near the clock to
observe.*

> MERLE

I don't think the station insurance covers this.
Actually, I don't think there is any station
insurance.

*Art places the ladder beneath the clock
and starts to climb. Gwen rushes over to
steady the ladder.*

> GWEN

You don't need to do this. It won't make a
difference. The train will come when it comes.

He climbs down.

> ART

It makes a difference. Not to the train, no. But
it makes a difference.

She nods.

> GWEN

I guess it does. Go for it!

He climbs the ladder.

ART
Hold it steady. I'm going to have to use the top step.

GWEN
Merle, would you help me, please?

Merle sidles up to the ladder and grabs one side, while she grabs the other.

ART
Got it?

GWEN
Got it.

Arts reaches up, slips his hand behind the clock and finds the knob.

ART
What time is it now?

GWEN
Hold on.

She reaches down for her phone. The ladder sways. Art flattens himself against the wall and holds on.

GWEN
Three fourteen and a little.

He twists the knob clockwise, but the hands go backward.

He twists it counterclockwise, and the hands spin forward, finally reaching three fourteen.

Art climbs carefully down the ladder and reaches the floor.

They all stare up at the clock, hoping it will move.

Nothing happens.

Then Merle walks to the wall and flips a switch.

The second hand starts to turn.

MERLE

They turned it off in 2011. The clock always ran fast anyway.

Art turns to Gwen.

ART

They usually do.

She smiles.

A train whistle sounds.

GWEN
That's my train. I hope.

ART
Do you?

GWEN
Less than I did before.

She rushes back to the bench, begins collecting her things.

He follows.

ART
I'm glad I got to see you again.

Gwen glances at the clock.

GWEN
You are still an interesting man.

Then she frowns.

GWEN
Wait.

He gets a hopeful look on his face.

ART
What?

GWEN
The world is a sphere.

ART
So?

GWEN
The surface of a sphere is an arc.

ART
And?

GWEN
So trains travel in arcs.

*Art lifts his head again, thinking, then
glances at the clock.*

ART
I'll think I'll buy a ticket.

She stops collecting, looks at him.

GWEN
Why?

*Art turns to Merle, who has retreated to
his cart.*

ART
Hey Merle?

MERLE
Yes?

ART
Do you have baseball caps for sale?

MERLE
Yeah, sure. Yankees. Red Sox. Mets. That's
from 1986.

Art walks over to the cart.

ART
86 Mets? That's perfect. How much?

*Merle looks at the hat as if it is an old
friend. Then he hands it to Art.*

MERLE
Take it. You're doing me a Favor.

Art comes back and offers it to Gwen.

*She hesitates, then spins her hair into a
ponytail and puts on the cap.*

Art steps back.

ART
Perfect. And there's one more reason.

Gwen adjusts the hat.

GWEN
Which is?

Art picks up her bags.

ART
I need to check out this arc thing. Could be a whole new old world.

GWEN
But you don't know where I'm going.

Art shrugs, this one with deep humor.

ART
Here to there. Where else is there?

She pauses, then slowly nods.

GWEN
Let's find out.

She turns to Merle.

GWEN
Thank you, Merle. See you next trip.

They hear the train pulling in.

Gwen and Art exit together under the clock and through the doors to the station platform.

Merle sits back on his stool and takes up the crossword again.

MERLE

(Spelling it out).

Unusual, rare, or extraordinary. U-N-W-O-N-T-E-D.

He stops, ponders, looks at the double doors to the track, then up at the clock, where the second hand is now sweeping along.

MERLE

Must have been the mints.

STEPHEN EVANS

ABOUT THE PLAYWRIGHT

Stephen Evans is a playwright and author. Find him online at:

https://www.istephenevans.com/

https://www.facebook.com/iStephenEvans

https://www.gr8word.com

STEPHEN EVANS

BOOKS BY STEPHEN EVANS

Fiction:

The Island of Always Series:

    The Marriage of True Minds

    Let Me Count the Ways

    My Winter World

Whose Beauty is Past Change

The Marriage Gift

Paradox

The Mind of a Writer and other Fables

Epigrammaticon

The Next Joy and the Next: A Mythology

Non-Fiction:

Prolegomena to Any Future Vacation

Funny Thing Is: A Guide to Understanding Comedy

The Laughing String: Thoughts on Writing

Layers of Life: Essays and Aphorisms

Liebestraum

Plays:

The Visitation Quartet:

> *The Ghost Writer*
>
> *Spooky Action at a Distance*
>
> *Tourists*
> Monuments

At the Still Point

Generations	(with Morey Norkin and Michael Gilles)
As You Like It	(by William Shakespeare, adapted by Stephen Evans)
The Glass Door	(An Adaptation of *Hedda Gabler* by Henrik Ibsen))

Verse:

Limerosity

Limerositus

Sonets from the Chesapeke

A Look from Winter

STEPHEN EVANS

STEPHEN EVANS